ACHIEVING PUBLICATION IN EDUCATION

John Eggleston and Gillian Klein

Warwick Papers on Education No. 7

Trentham Books

ACHIEVING PUBLICATION IN EDUCATION

First published in 1997 by Trentham Books Limited

Trentham Books Limited
Westview House
734 London Road
Oakhill
Stoke on Trent
Staffordshire
England ST4 5NP

British Cataloguing in Publication Data
A catalogue record for this book is available from the British Library
ISBN: 1 85856 066 7

Designed and typeset by Trentham Print Design Ltd., Chester
and printed in Great Britain by Bemrose Shafron Ltd., Chester

Contents

Acknowledgements

This pamphlet is based on the authors' experiences as writers, editors, referees, publishers and consultants. We are indebted to countless colleagues with whom we have worked and in particular to the many authors whose work has passed across our desks.

We are also grateful to the British Educational Research Association for its endeavours to encourage and support writers and are glad to acknowledge the rich source of quotations we have tapped from issue No 56 of *Research Intelligence,* one of BERA's journals. We commend the Association to our readers.

John Eggleston and Gillian Klein

Introduction

Writing for publication has always been an important and necessary activity for academics and other professionals. It constitutes the main instrument whereby knowledge, understanding and interpretation is developed, established and communicated. Although print has now been augmented by a range of electronic media, the format of the message itself is largely unchanged from traditional print and the print on paper format is still the most frequent end product of all but the most ephemeral and unselective of electronic communications. The enduring nature of print is demonstrated by the burgeoning numbers of new books and journals in every field of academic and professional activity. Indeed it is almost axiomatic that a field of study cannot claim to be established unless it has amassed a significant body of publication, if not a specifically dedicated journal.

In the circumstances the present concern and renewed emphasis on the need to publish seems surprising. Surely the surprising thing is that many professionals and, particularly, academics have published little or even, as recent surveys have shown, nothing at all. The present strong emphasis on publication by university and higher education staff – with its implications for funding, promotion and tenure – are best seen as a heavy-handed and crude way of rectifying a situation. Although the pressure on staff in further education establishments and schools is less heavy, there is no doubt that a strong track record of publication has important and powerful value in career enhancement.

But writing for publication is difficult. Good lectures and seminars do not necessarily translate well to published form. Research findings require precise and skilful treatment if their importance is to be communicated to fellow specialists or to the wider world. Yet unless this is done they are virtually worthless. This pamphlet sets out to provide practical help to professionals working in educational studies in universities and higher and further education, to teachers in schools and colleges and to researchers.

No attempt is made to discuss the publication of 'textbooks' specifically designed for students' use because such books seldom offer original material and it is usually only their structure and organisation that is new, not their content. Their purpose is often rather more commercial than academic professional publications can hope to be – although there are notable exceptions.

Similarly, we do not offer advice on electronic publishing. A useful guide to this is available from the Authors' Licencing and Collecting Society, 74 New Oxford Street, London WC1A 1EF, entitled *Guidelines for Writers in Electronic Publishing and Multimedia*.

Achieving Publication in Education is concerned with writing that determines the furtherance and dissemination of knowledge and understanding about education. It offers concise advice about content, style, choice of publication, submissions, the complexities of refereeing, citations, editorial decisions and other factors that influence the chances of success or failure.

CHAPTER I

What to write about

If you haven't anything worth saying don't write about it. This is an axiom frequently ignored by journalists with space to fill and punitive deadlines. Alas, it is also often ignored by academics and other professional writers. Certainly many authors, faced with intense pressure to publish, search desperately for topics to write about.

Yet the search need not and should not create anguish, still less give rise to desperate measures. Every researcher must produce results, of a hypothesis either validated or nullified, and unless the original hypothesis was totally misconceived or pointless then surely there are publishable results. The classic research dilemma is, however, whether to wait until final results are available. And as in much educational research there is no unambiguous finality, it can be that completion and publication recede over the horizon. If the present pressures for publications lead to the finalisation of a few more research projects they will not have been in vain.

A publication about an interesting research topic need not wait until the project ends. Interim results can be of great professional importance and their publication, along with indications of next steps, can be particularly valuable. Such exposure can engage other professionals in the field to offer suggestions and alert the researcher to relevant current work elsewhere, thereby enhancing the prospects of the project. Writing about the research methodology being developed or applied can be equally valid and rewarding.

For those who specialise in teaching rather than research the quest for a topic may seem more difficult. Yet there can be few teachers who, if not already involved in formulating curriculum policy, have not developed their own particular approaches to and interpretations of the subjects they teach and evaluated them in the tough reality of lecture room and classroom. The school improvement movement has given new impetus to action research by teachers. Articles reporting new professional practices and offering examples of actual teaching and students' responses are likely to be of great interest to other professionals, whose comments can again bring added reward. Practitioner journals ensure that new work of this kind can be promptly published.

A related source of writing topics comes from the organisation and management of teaching and new developments in pedagogy. Just one new aspect of teaching arrangements – the mentoring of teacher-training students in schools and similar initiatives in industries and the social sciences – has led to the establishment of a new professional journal and generated a flood of highly targeted and publishable articles from teachers and researchers involved in the process.

Whatever the topic, any writing for publication should be original or, in media terms, be 'news'. It should not be a regurgitation of old ideas, methodologies or common knowledge already possessed by potential readers. However, originality need not be too formidable a hurdle. Although writing about doctoral research, Phillips and Pugh (1994) were able, drawing from a range of sources, to list 15 different ways of being original. These are:

- setting down a major piece of new information in writing for the first time

- continuing a previously original piece of work

- carrying out original work designed by a senior colleague

- providing a single original technique, observation or result in an otherwise unoriginal but competent piece of research

- having many original ideas, methods and interpretations all performed by others under the direction of the writer

- showing originality in testing somebody else's idea

- carrying out empirical work that hasn't been done before

- making a synthesis that hasn't been made before

- using already known material but with a new interpretation

- trying out something in this country that has previously only been done in other countries

- taking a particular known technique and applying it in a new area

- bringing new evidence to bear on an old issue

- being cross-disciplinary and using different methodologies

- looking at areas that people in the discipline haven't looked at before

- adding to knowledge in a way that hasn't previously been done before.

To this extensive list we would add:

*   making connections between different disciplines or different areas of one discipline that have not been made before.

As Phillips and Pugh conclude: 'This should be reassuring. It is much easier to be original in at least one of fifteen possible ways that it is to be singularly original.' Salmon's collection of student experiences (1992) shows some of the many ways this advice can be used.

Not all articles emanate from the professional work done by authors. An important *genre* of article is the rejoinder or critique of already published articles in the learned and professional press. These may simply be a direct and substantial rebuttal of the article which is being responded to but it is often used as a peg on which to hang a range of the challenger's own ideas which in themselves would not have been enough to achieve publication.

Journal editors tend to look favourably on rejoinders if they are submitted promptly after the substantive article has appeared – they bring a spark of controversy to what may be a rather staid publication. And it shows that somebody out there is not only reading the journal but also responding to it actively and seriously. But most of all it gives an unknown author a chance to topple the mighty and become mighty themselves in the process. The fall of Sir Cyril Burt was a classic example of such power, although the writers of the rejoinders are now themselves being widely rejoindered. Writing for publication is a potent instrument of power and needs to be treated with respect.

Only the mainstream, recurring sources of themes have been mentioned so far. There are many others of interest. Articles on the closures or mergers of departments, the implications of financial cuts, student initiatives, the implications of government policies – these and many more can have significant effects on teaching and research and can lead to published work. Such articles may be more akin to journalism; the line between journalistic articles and academic articles is a fine one and becoming ever more blurred. And articles in the serious broadsheets or weeklies, although still rated only marginally in research assessment exercises, can have a highly beneficial role in enhancing the standing of the author, department and institution from which they come.

A common starting point for articles is a PhD thesis or Masters' dissertation. If the study is successful it is possible that several articles can be generated. It can even be the basis for a book – if adapted as suggested in Chapter 4. Careful editing and rewriting are essential. An individual chapter of a thesis removed from its original context is unlikely to be, in itself, a valid article. Extensive rewriting, using only the relevant parts of the literature search and the relevant parts of the conclusion, are virtually essential. The PhD and Masters' dissertation are one form of publication; journal articles and professional articles are something else. Skilful re-packaging is all-important. If you are really far-sighted you will decide which articles you wish to write and construct your thesis around the articles. But this is a sophisticated double-take that few aspire to and even fewer achieve.

The purpose of this chapter has been simple; to refute the argument that anybody in education has nothing worth writing about. We now go on to suggest how it might be written.

References

Phillips, E M and Pugh, D S (1994) *How to get a PhD*, 2nd Edition, Buckingham: Open University Press

Salmon, P (1992) *Achieving a PhD*, Stoke-on-Trent: Trentham Books

CHAPTER 2

How to target a journal and write for it

When writing for a learned journal, study the aspired publication carefully to identify the topics that recur regularly, to identify the editorial idiosyncrasies, to steep yourself in the language, to become familiar with the preferred style. Then prepare the article within that context.

Identifying your target journal or publisher

This crucial process assumes a knowledge of likely journals in the relevant fields. Most burgeoning authors will be familiar with many of them; it is essential to check the contents carefully so that existing articles may be related to and cited where appropriate. An evident familiarity with the way the journal has represented the chosen area in recent issues is highly desirable, even essential.

New journals are constantly appearing and existing ones are being relaunched and rejigged. Even the best informed author might be unaware of a relevant journal, especially if it is published in another country. Checking with librarians can usually help; for an exhaustive search Blackwell's Serial Catalogue, published annually mid-year, is a reliable and fairly comprehensive guide. In education, libraries will have access to ERIC –

the Education Research Information Center database in America – which is virtually exhaustive.

Many attempts have been made to achieve a full list of education journals. But even to list those in the English language is a formidable task; there are vast numbers and they change constantly. Moreover education is a diffuse, broad area of study; many articles on education could equally well appear in journals in a wide range of adjacent areas. However it is rumoured that the British Education Research Association is about to attempt this heroic task – watch their publications.

If an unknown journal is chosen the same rules about familiarity apply before writing begins. If one is targeting a first issue the odds are unfavourable: most new journals 'pack' their first few issues with commissioned articles by established authors in their fields – often the editorial board.

Journals fall into well-defined categories. First are the wide ranging 'discipline' journals such as *Sociology, British Journal of Psychology, Nature* – all of which publish articles on education. Then there are the numerous specialist journals in education such as the *British Journal of the Sociology of Education*, and the *International Journal of Early Years Education*. In a third category are the 'sectoral' publications such as the *British Journal of Counselling and Guidance*, usually with a narrow and more highly focused field. Yet a fourth category covers the practitioners' journals, in which the criteria for acceptance are more strongly related to illumination and support for professionals rather than the direct enhancement of scholarship in the field. Examples include the NATE journal, *Education in English*, and the TACTYC journal *Early Years*. Many of these may be available as membership journals to professional organisations. A final category would be 'newspapers', notably the three *Times* supplements (*Educational,*

Higher Education and *Literary*), the *New Yorker* and more serious broadsheet newspapers world-wide such as the *New York Times*, *The Age,* the *Financial Times* and many others.

The obvious hierarchy of newspapers opens the issue of the general hierarchy of publications. The crucial distinction is 'peer appraisal': wherein all the articles submitted are sent out to known specialists for comment before any decision is made about acceptance. This is widely regarded as the most demanding test and thus a major indication of the quality of the content of the journal. So it is seen as probably the most important indication of quality by university Research Assessment Exercises and by a wide range of academic appoint-ment and promotion committees. The first three categories of publication described are almost all conducted on peer review; many of the professional journals are assessed in the same way and usually indicate if this is their practice. However, the stringent editorial selection of many newspapers and magazines is well known and their quality rating is well recognised; their selection is arguably more rigorous than some peer review procedures.

Peer review, however, is not the only important criterion. Some journals are notoriously hard to get into. These are usually the long established wide spectrum discipline journals such as the *American Journal of Sociology* or more specialist journals such as the *British Journal of Educational Research*, which are regularly overloaded with contributors. But the ratings are volatile; great journals can decline and new ones triumph. Much the same is true of the more 'popular' publications; to obtain a slot in *Nature* or the *Economist* is equally difficult.

Another key indicator of journal quality is the extent to which its articles are cited. And as the number and quality and source of positive citations of a published article is so important, to target a widely cited journal is an appropriate choice for an ambitious

9

author. But high ambition equals high risk and the choice of target requires sensitive judgement by any author.

As we shall discuss in Chapter 4, criteria for books are similar. Here, too, there is a hierarchy of publishers: the major international university presses are usually seen as top of the pecking order, notably Oxford, Harvard and Cambridge, which are usually regarded as highly selective. Not surprisingly they are sharply aware of the commercial significance of their decisions. Within Oxford University Press an elite and much aspired to imprint is the Clarendon Press. Other major international publishers, Macmillan, Wiley and others, also have extensive and well regarded lists and offer a high degree of quality assurance. Many other, more recently established publishers, such as the Open University Press and Trentham Books are highly regarded in their specialist fields and have achieved distinctive and esteemed lists.

Many publishers of books on education have series of books in areas such as Special Educational Needs, Counselling and Guidance and other special areas. These are usually edited by specialists in their field who, as part of their role, are able to guide and advise potential authors. This is particularly useful for those who are attempting a book for the first time. They, too, usually seek peer referees and operate a similar process to the major journals. Some publishers also produce series of pamphlets which can claim the attention and respect accorded full-length books. Most publishers of education books produce, at various times, edited collections of papers, usually put together by a senior figure in the field but which might provide a vehicle for less well known authors who have something important to say. This half-way house between journal and full book publication offers a useful starting point for academic and professional writing careers.

The size and strength of journal publishers is also something to reckon with; major stables such as Carfax, Blackwell, Taylor and Francis, and Kluwer are well organised to deliver 'market penetration' of their titles and therefore to enhance the exposure and citation enjoyed by authors of the articles they contain.

Meeting the standards

Every journal will have a set of guidelines for contributors – either published with each issue or available on request. As part of these guides many journals require authors to submit an outline of their article before a final version. Heed this advice; it may save long hours of pointless effort and yield useful early guidance and even advantage. To write a compelling outline is itself a demanding task and requires the author to display coherence, initiative, imagination and organised thinking.

Articles that satisfy the given guidelines have a consistently greater chance of success. This is particularly true of guidelines concerning length and citation style. Editors can become infuriated if a submitted article has to be re-edited throughout to change every reference to the standard format of the journal. Moreover, editors may suspect not just indolence but also that the article has been prepared in the style of a competing journal and then rejected by that journal. The hard truth is that articles rejected by one journal may have to be recast – even fundamentally – before submission elsewhere. Understandably, editors consider articles on the assumption that they will be able to publish them if they accept them. The penalties of concurrent or multiple submissions are dire. Many specialist journals have overlapping teams of referees so the crime is frequently detected. The penalty can well be a covert ban on material from that author being considered again. In a word: **'don't'**.

There are two other actions that can lead to a life-time ban. One is plagiarism, a sin for which there is no forgiveness. Even the most scrupulous referees sometimes fail to detect it, but sooner or later a hawk-eyed reader – often the author of the plagiarised material – will recognise it, and the mandatory public apology will ensure that the plagiarisers are disgraced in their own professional community. And if, in the years before discovery, they have attained high professional status, the price can be horrendous.

The second peril is the spoof article. It's an exciting, daring act of bravado to make fools of editors and referees and then publicise their folly. But the long-term price is suspicion and defensiveness about anything you write in future. The saga of Alan Sokal's spoof article for a leading American cultural studies journal has been extensively reported (Ross, 1996) and is on its way to becoming a cautionary legend.

Issues of style

Whichever journal is targeted, there are basic rules which apply to all submissions. One of the most important is style. Clarity, logic, accuracy and precision are crucial. What is required is not memorable literature but effective communication. Yet the style of a good lecture or even a TV or radio presentation is usually inappropriate. Spoken communication often needs to achieve a continuous flow of words, and has a reliance on context that is inappropriate in a scholarly or even professional article.

Headings and sub-headings are important to guide the readers through the article. Adopt the style of the journal you target, which will have its own 'hierarchy' of heading styles.

It is easier to define bad writing than good. Vocabulary will be limited, ridden with cliché and jargon; sentences gratuitously complicated or convoluted. It may all be grammatically correct but turgid, flat and boring. Some authors mistrust their readers and don't credit them with the ability to connect the ideas proposed in sentence one with what follows in sentence two, but tell it all over again.

There is no one kind of good writing, but there are certain identifiable qualities that contribute to good informative writing. Communicating clearly, as we stress repeatedly, is the first criterion. A wide vocabulary, a sense of rhythm and pace, liven the prose and hold the reader's attention. Occasional humour and a few vivid metaphors to lock notions in the reader's mind will be appreciated. However complex and demanding the content, a good writer will make it accessible. Just read how Steve Jones puts across complex information on genetics in *In the Blood* (1996) for an example.

Good writing is best learned from 'good' reading, which is probably why English Literature graduates so often become successful writers. Reading in the discipline of education is riskier: some authors in the field write well, even rivetingly, but others plod heavily. Good writing also comes with practice. Certainly fluency comes easier with each project, but only if you keep a clear sense of whom you are writing for, a sense of your audience and what they will find most accessible and interesting, rather than becoming enchanted with the 'sound of your own voice' on the page.

There should be no need to preface any sentence with 'it is a fact that...' – if it is not a fact it should not be included. The same applies to 'it is important to point out that'. Moderation on emphases is also prudent; adjectives such as significant, important and crucial can soon become discredited. Advertisers have long recognised this problem; academic writers need to recognise it too. Another stylistic error is to make sweeping statements such as 'it is well known that'. If a point is important it is best substantiated by one or more references, otherwise international readers of journals will be disadvantaged by the localised knowledge and assumptions of the author.

Many writers seem to assume that in order to indicate extreme profundity or wisdom the style must be obscure or even impenetrable. This is fallacious. Many articles are rejected by all publications – even the most specialist – simply because they are likely to be inaccessible to their readers. David Budge (1996) quotes a prize example which was actually published in *Changing English*:

> This paper has contested Hunter's Foucauldian account of the hidden 'real' historical explanation of the formation of the literary subject as a (state-sanctioned) quest to re-unify the divided problematised aesthetic-ethical self in English.

It may, on the other hand, be that the point which you are thinking of making is so likely to be part of the general knowledge of the readers of the specialist journal that it is unnecessary even to mention it. Over a quarter of the submissions for the first two years for the journal *Mentoring and Tutoring* included several pages explaining the Socratic origins of the term 'Mentoring' – already familiar to virtually every reader of the journal.

Genderised language is a problem. In the past it was acceptable to attribute maleness to the impersonal pronoun. For example, 'when a pupil experiences a problem **he** is encouraged to consult **his** teacher. **He** will be able to help **him**.' Now it may be seen as exclusionist. Many journals have specific conventions on style in this matter. Some are clumsy, like the use of 'he and she' or even 's/he' throughout. Others redress the balance by using she throughout, which can be confusing. Perhaps the simplest solution is to use plural forms and restrict gender pronouns to individual cases where the gender of the subject is identified. Failing this, person or young person can be substituted for man or woman, boy or girl. While it may be easy to edit in this way and to avoid out-moded clichés such as 'separating the men from the boys', it is much harder to eliminate the hidden gender assumptions that are built into contemporary culture. Only skilful editing – perhaps helped by a colleague – can achieve this. Implicitly exclusive assumptions apply equally to ethnic issues. Assuming that all pupils – or all teachers – are white is as exclusionist as using language which suggests that all are male. There is probably no aspect of scholarship in which such sensitivity is more important than the study of education.

Consistency of argument is all-important. Articles should begin with a crisp abstract of the piece and proceed to a well substantiated conclusion, with the way signposted by sharp and consistently presented sub-headings. There should be no place for distracting asides or marginal examples, however keenly the author wishes to share them.

Once the first draft is achieved the author needs to edit for style (some writers might augment this sentence with 'in his or her own way' but this is wholly unnecessary and clumsy). Editing involves careful checking of grammar, including correct use of apostrophes, the efficacy of the spell-checker used and, above all, clarity. Subject should always agree with verb and the use of relative clauses that break up sentences should be controlled. For example, remember that words such as none and everyone are singular and require a singular verb. Words should be used for their precision not their length: 'try' does as well as 'endeavour'. Sloppy or verbose writing is not appreciated by editors – or by readers. When in doubt, it is worth consulting one of the ultimate style bibles: Gowers (1986), Fowler (Burchfield, 1996) or *The Oxford Guide to English Usage* (Weiner and Delahunty, 1993), which can almost always help. Should present readers find such details trivial or even pedantic we recommend that they read the preface to Julian Barnes' *Letters from London* (1995), in which he describes the working of the twin terrors of the *New Yorker* editorial process. These are the 'style police' and the 'fact checking department', whose 'operatives are young, unsleeping, scrupulously polite and astoundingly pertinacious'. By comparison the stringency, explicit and implicit, outlined in this booklet will appear relaxed and even benign. But careless spelling or punctuation, or poor grammar is hardly an advertisement for scholarly thinking.

Check consistencies in all style details, however minor. Either first names of all cited authors should be given or only initials, otherwise there may be an implication of favouritism, patronage or, even worse, gender bias. Even on such apparently trivial matters such as consistency in using eg or e.g., precision is needed. To have to edit to ensure this consistency throughout an author's submission may be the last straw for a busy editor and lead to a rejection slip that could have been averted.

Joint authorship of articles

So far this chapter has assumed sole authorship. Yet many researchers and teachers work in groups and teams and a jointly authored publication is an appropriate way of dividing the labour and the credit. The division of labour can take various forms: each partner can work up a section, one can draft the entire piece and the others revise; there are many permutations. Whatever strategy is adopted, good, harmonious personal relationships and agreements on approach are essential. In-fighting is the enemy of a successful piece of work, and friendships have turned to enmity over a single article. And there is one further hazard – in most citation indices it is the first-named author who makes the listings, the rest being assumed anonymously as *et al*. If in a mood of democratic egalitarianism the authors list themselves alphabetically then the A, B and Cs have it and the X, Y and Zs are likely to be relegated to anonymity. So accreditation needs to be negotiated to everyone's satisfaction at the outset. The subtleties of accreditation are discussed in detail in Chapter 4 (p.35-36).

As a final tie-up, check back to the introduction and see how well it relates to the concluding paragraph. The match should be perfect and the argument developed with a logical link between them. Finally, revise the abstract to bring out the outstanding quality of what has been achieved so that the immediate reaction of the receiving editor will be a frisson of keen expectation.

References

Budge, D (1996) 'Working with the Press, 3' *Research Intelligence* No 56

Burchfield, R W (1996) *The New Fowler's Modern English Usage 3rd ed.* Oxford: Clarendon Press

Barnes, J (1995) *Letters from London.* London: Picador

Gowers, E (revised edition, 1986) *The Complete Plain Words.* London: HMSO

Jones, S (1996) *In the Blood.* London: Harper Collins

Ross, A (1996) 'Burden of Spoof' *Times Higher Education Supplement,* June 21

Weiner, E S C and Delahunty, A (1993) *Oxford Guide to English Usage 2nd ed.* Oxford: University Press

CHAPTER 3

Submitting your work

If the author has fulfilled all the steps outlined in the previous chapter the prospects of success should be greatly enhanced. But there are still some technicalities to consider.

The article must be impeccably wordprocessed, with double spacing and wide margins and presented on one side only of each sheet of A4 paper. (Disks are only needed on acceptance.) Referees and editors may need space on which to comment as they read and edit; appearance also counts. The required number of copies to be supplied is usually three but might be more. The author's name, affiliation and address should appear on a separate title sheet which can be detached to facilitate the anonymity of the refereeing process. After submitting this polished piece, the author will usually obtain an acknowledgement from the editorial office. It could take weeks or even months before further news is received. Nothing can happen until the editor has received comments from all the referees contacted. When these are received, negotiations between editor and referees may follow and, in case of doubt, further referees could be consulted. Finally, possibly at a meeting of the editorial board, a decision will be made and the author informed. The decision can take several possible forms:

- Outright acceptance – rare but not unknown – usually with a publication date specified which may be up to several years ahead

- Outright rejection – usually accompanied by an explanation which offers suggestions for revision or alternative destinations which the editor or the referees believe to be more appropriate

- A critique of the article suggesting how, with revision, it can be resubmitted to the journal for consideration. This will often include anonymous extracts from a referee's report. If you receive such a response it is usually well worth following up carefully and promptly. It is an indication that the half-way mark has been achieved – a kind of author's purgatory.

What can the author do to enhance success in this often long drawn out process? The basic strategies are clear. Most editors have to find a quick way to identify suitable referees. A common strategy is to search through the author's citations to find known authorities which the writer has used and to invite those writers to referee. This gives the writer a good chance to influence the choice of referee. It follows that it is particularly prudent to ensure that correct identification is given, with correctly quoted relevant extracts that are well used, argued and substantiated. Inaccurate quotation and unsubstantiated critical argument are very likely to lead to a negative view from any referees quoted. This is not to say that authors should be deferential or subservient to famous authors they cite; indeed most referees are prepared to accept and encourage a well substantiated challenge to their views and may prefer it to obsequious acquiescence. It is also useful to remember that most editors use their own editorial board extensively as referees; study the published list carefully and, if appropriate, acquaint yourself with and use their work.

Yet another strategy is to submit not a final article but a well developed outline and ask for advice and guidance. We have already noted that an outline is required by some journals. Even if it is not, this can be an extremely useful way of getting good general advice and picking up the orientations of some of the anonymous referees, who are very likely to be asked to look at the article again when it is finally submitted. A positive response is a very useful foot in the door and a negative response at least saves the author from further high risk efforts with the same journal.

If an author is invited to submit, it is prudent to do so promptly – if only to protect your slot in the take-off line and to ensure that you have not slipped out of the editor's consciousness. Try to get it right; it is unusual to give authors a second chance to submit; life is short and editors are busy.

Don't hassle the editor in an attempt to achieve early publication. If editors see a case for accelerated publication they would expect to make that decision independently. Unless there is a desperate need for revision after acceptance do not attempt to revise. The article may already be set in proof; your intervention may cause it to be pulled out of line and again lose its take-off slot. If editors have made major deletions, even of your most carefully crafted pages, do not attempt to re-insert. Space may be short or the editor may know that the material being deleted has been covered elsewhere, possibly in an article already accepted for the same journal or even the same issue.

Practitioners' journals

It would be a mistake to discount the value of publishing articles in the well-respected practitioners' journals. Instead of a circulation of only a few hundred (with very few exceptions) you can expect a circulation of thousands. And the very fact that the subscribers expect the journal to enhance their professional practice means that your piece is likely to be read. So if your aim is not just academic validation but also a concern to improve education, the appropriate practitioner journal, the teachers' union periodicals, or even general magazines like *Junior Education* are the appropriate vehicles for your ideas. Moreover, certain of these journals are widely cited: look for instance at books about education and race and you will find a significant number of articles cited from *MCT – Multicultural Teaching*.

The piece you submit, however, will have to be quite different in style from those you write for the refereed journals. Your audience is teachers – although academics also read these journals. The editor has a sense of the practitioner in school or college. So a more direct, even journalistic tone is called for. Nonetheless, arguments have to be validated by research, citations must be scholarly, and the style of the journal regarding citations and layout must be followed.

Not only are good practitioner journals widely read and often widely cited, they may also be more accessible. Even if papers go to referees, the editor will be likely to take pieces that are not up to standard in their writing if what they say is new, exciting and relevant. Editors are also prepared to consider work based on practical experience or experiential learning, although they will expect the authors to back up their own observations with the literature – where it exists. So while new research goes to refereed journals, new **ideas** can first be worked out in practitioner journals. Again taking *MCT* as our example, this and other journals are deliberately extending authorship to teachers and to those whose voice is least heard in education, as opposed to the rather 'clubby' authorship of academic journals in certain fields.

If the editor of the practitioner journal is prepared to 'blue-pencil' your submission because you views and ideas are significant, you will learn a good deal about how an article should be written. And at any event, seeing your piece presented in a professional journal will boost your confidence, and being seen in it may well enhance your career.

Armed with the eventual acceptance note and assurance of publication, the final step is to consolidate and build on your success. A final chapter will help you to do this; read on.

CHAPTER 4

Writing a Book

The best reason for writing a book is because you have been commissioned to do so. You are approached by a publisher or, increasingly more likely, an academic colleague who knows your area of expertise, has evidence that you can write and who is putting together a series for a publisher.

The next best reason is that you have something new and useful to communicate and that it requires a whole book to do so. Although many books are published that do not meet this requirement they are almost certainly written by people who already know their way round the market and are known in it. First-time book authors have to convince a publisher that:

- their book really does say something new, topical and marketable

- that they are the person to write it and are capable of doing so, preferably to a deadline.

On no account write your book *before* you have a publisher. Apart from the obvious waste of time and energy – even a fairly short book, say 50,000 words, takes close to a year from planning to indexing – pre-written manuscripts are actually *less* attractive to publishers. A good in-house editor will have a sense of readership potential and a sense of the market, that you as author need to know and write for. A book is for being read but many first-time authors do not consult their editors about how to attract and interest an audience.

Never send an entire manuscript unsolicited – it is an embarrassment to the publisher. Moreover, should it fall into the wrong hands, it could be plagiarised and you would find it difficult to make a case for ownership.

Making a book proposal

1. *Planning it*

At the outset, remember that if publishers accept a book they have to invest at least £10,000 ($15,000) in you at their risk. So they need a good deal of persuasion. The first step is to compile a polished, professional book proposal targeted at a particular publisher (with perhaps a couple of possible alternatives in mind). Sending a generalised proposal to a whole range of publishers is unlikely to interest any of them. Choose a publisher with whom you are familiar, whose books you read, whose list covers the areas in which you are interested and to which your work contributes. That way you will be more likely to approximate to the pitch – the appropriate register for an audience of which you yourself are part – and the style of the house. And the commissioning editor will be able to see a 'fit' with the list, which is advantageous in marketing.

All publishers are to some extent looking for the same thing:

- a new idea, new research with implications for practice

- a new interpretation or perspective on a currently topical subject – but this has to be significantly new

- a book that will sell, which requires a broad-based readership and/or offers 'essential' material

- a book that is accurate, authoritative, balanced and (reasonably) comprehensive

- straightforward writing, or better still, lively straight-forward writing – let Fowler (see p.17) be your guide. No editor is likely to confuse obfuscation and pretentious style with authoritativeness or complex thought

- a theme that won't pass its 'sell-by' date until two years later – at least.

2. Content

Your book proposal should give the prospective publisher the following information about your book:

a. What it is about.

b. How it relates to the existing literature: It is important not to fudge – editors know their market and want to be sure that you know the field too. Ignoring the competition could be taken as ignorance of its existence. Say why your book is different from or better than existing books.

c. Who the book is for:

the perceived readership

why those readers will want it

ways in which you, the author, will activate that market (influencing student reading lists, presenting papers at conferences, giving guest lectures and ensuring reviews).

d. Format: Indicate your length – and try to stick to it! Publishers prefer 60,000 words to 100,000 and are reluctant to consider anything longer without convincing reasons. Costs of publishing are an important factor. Photographs are expensive, especially if in colour and should be avoided unless absolutely essential. Copyright material from other published work can require expensive fees for permission to use, especially if from American sources, and is best avoided. If it is used, publishers will usually charge the author for the fees. Original diagrams and charts are not a problem if supplied 'camera ready' by the author but the space they occupy must be allowed for in the word count.

e. Delivery: Specify the date of completion, backed up with a brief picture of where you are with the material, what time your schedule allows for writing, your productivity level.

You can support your case in a number of ways. It is a good idea to include a sample of your writing – ideally an offprint of an academic article by you in a refereed journal. If you cannot produce this, include a sample from a section of your proposed book – many publishers only make a decision after reading a sample chapter. They need reassurance that you can write. Give some information about yourself that affirms your knowledge of your subject, how you are regarded in the field, your professional post. It may be helpful to cite one or two referees (especially if they are authors on the publisher's list!) but only if you have arranged this with them in advance. A referee might also write a brief endorsement of you and your project. All this is particularly useful if you are recasting an academic study, say a PhD, as a book – discussed later in this section.

Remember that your proposal has added value if you can provide evidence that you yourself will be able to help to sell the book and not be diffident about promoting it.

THE PROPOSAL

Introduction
A paragraph on each of the following:

a. the overall scope and content, with title or working title and likely length and format

b. how it relates to the existing market

c. who will read it; who will buy it

d. your professional position/authoritativeness in the subject

e. Predicted date of completion (allow yourself a few months' leeway)

A Synopsis – Chapter outline – a line or two on each chapter's contents (you can give chapter headings, if you have them). Main conclusions – a brief indication.

A sample of your writing

Names of referees

Strategies

Write, if you can, to a named person in the house – more publishers now identify their editors in their catalogues. It is even better if you can establish contact first, either at a book exhibition at say, a BERA or AERA conference, or by telephone. Publishers often trawl universities and conferences seeking authors; this indicates that they are in need of new titles so your chances of success are good. Proposals have nevertheless been known to sit on editors' desks for long periods: you do not want yours to get 'lost' or go cold. So after a month enquire calmly, after two months become more strident and after six months walk away with your proposal. If your first choice of publisher has rejected it, try elsewhere quickly. If possible, ask for a debriefing in case of refusal. Be sure to keep a copy of all you send. Always include a stamped self-addressed envelope of sufficient size with your submission.

At the publishers

When a viable proposal is eventually received at the publisher's office referees will usually be consulted. You may influence the choice of referees by suggesting names, although publishers will usually ensure that at least one is independent. (Book referees, unlike journal referees, are usually paid a small fee.)

When the publisher is satisfied a contract will be issued. This is a lengthy document specifying the most unlikely issues – such as film and cartoon rights of your book or the merchandising of characters you have created. But it will tie you to a deadline, confirm the size of the book and offer you a royalty. For paperback books this is usually 7.5% or 8% of the price obtained by the publisher – usually 30-40% less than the cover price; even less for overseas sales. For hardbacks the figure is usually 10% but may rise to 12.5% when sales have exceeded a specified figure (which is seldom achieved). Advances on royalty are usually paid at two points – on final acceptance of the manuscript and then on publication. This, of course, diminishes subsequent royalty cheques. Sometimes publishers offer a flat 'once and for all' fee. For multi-authored books or collections this is logical; tiny royalties are difficult to administer. But never accept a flat fee for a single authored book. Otherwise you may see the book reach bestseller lists and have no share in the rich profits of your publisher! You should also check that you can claim a share of translation rights your publisher may negotiate; sometimes these can be highly rewarding.

It is always wise to seek a publisher who achieves good publicity – obtaining reviews, displaying at relevant conferences, targeted press advertising and a good 'presence' at relevant bookshops. Competition for sales becomes fiercer each year: Chapman and Hall were offering lecturers Air Miles (for free flights) at one time if they adopted Chapman and Hall books as required reading for their students. As yet there is no evidence of the efficacy of this campaign.

From proposal to book

Your publisher will have notes on *house style*, which should be carefully followed. They will deal with layout, headings and subheadings, quotations and the style of citations in text and bibliography.

Our advice would be to begin by only roughing out the *introduction*. However much a book is in your head, what you finally write is seldom precisely what you think you will write! Introductions are often best written near the end – perhaps just before you write the conclusion. Technology allows you to re-arrange chapter order but if you do, be sure to adjust any references you have made to what comes before or after.

Bibliography will be in line with house style but take care not to leave any references incomplete. You will have taken full bibliographic details of each source at the time you used it, and probably compiled your bibliography as you went along. There will be a chance to check at proof stage. No major western publisher sets in metal type any more, so minor changes are easily made at proof stage, by which time an in-house copy-editor will have worked through your text.

Indexing is only done on final proofs. Your publisher will arrange to have your book indexed if you wish but this is likely to cost you a minimum of £200. Advice on indexing your own book is offered on page 36.

As we have already mentioned, costs of *permissions* also have to be borne by the author. This is usually for anything more than ten consecutive lines of text, or for any picture, chart or diagram from a published work. It is usually best to approach the original publisher even when authors themselves own the copyright.

Title

You may have had one in mind all along, or the publisher may want a title that fits a series. Long titles are quickly forgotten so go for a short and, ideally, memorable one. Whatever you decide, you must keep in mind the databases and bibliographic sales services such as Book Data and Whitaker, and the library bibliographic search bases such as TES Bookfind, BBIP, ERIC, and Eurydice. These search by author and title but they also search by keywords. Keywords will be picked up as readily from the subtitle as the title but they *must* appear on the title page. Titles without relevant keywords, however ingenious, risk obscurity for your book.

Other bibliographic data will be supplied by the publisher: ISBN (international standard book number), price, date, size etc. All that remains to be done – should you choose to do so – is to write a brief paragraph of acknowledgements. You may even wish to acknowledge this pamphlet – but please do not! By then you will have incorporated anything that you find useful into your own consciousness.

Recasting a thesis

A Masters' degree is unlikely to be substantial enough to recast as a book. You may already have had an academic article or two from it but may well find, through your academic contacts, that it will also afford the material for a chapter in a book, or even a free-standing pamphlet like the Association for the Study of Primary Education papers.

A PhD is more likely to have the substance for a book but not every PhD is appropriate. The content has to be of reasonably wide interest and application and not too locked into fine detail. The requirement of originality in post-graduate research does, however, make PhDs potentially attractive and some publishers even court those engaged in doctoral theses.

To recast a PhD successfully major changes have to be made to:

1. **Voice**: A PhD has a clearly defined and tiny audience: your supervisor and the external examiner(s). All the writing is geared to satisfying those two or three people, and the perception of what will be satisfactory is determined by academic criteria. Many – such as accuracy, validity, relevance, logic, original thought, wide reading and avoidance of plagiarism – transfer automatically to the criteria for a good book. Others do not. Because a PhD has to be defended at a viva, the writing itself is defensive. One states, restates, overstates, justifies. One demonstrates that one knows what one is setting out to do and then that it has been done. The writing is puffed by 'it is necessary to...', 'given that such and such, it follows that...' . Additionally, many people learn how to write by doing their PhD and what they learn is often ponderous, verbose and deadly dull. The supervisor and the examiners have some familiarity with your topic and know how to skim. Even a well-written PhD is seldom crisp and direct.

Now your audience is a range of colleagues, some known but the vast majority unknown. You may also be targeting students and new entrants to education. You want them to read your book, not pick it up and then discard it. Points must be made unambiguously and concisely. The style should be clear, straightforward and, where possible, interesting and varied (see section on 'Issues of style' p.12-16). Sentences should not run on too long and each should flow to the next. Half a page is enough for the longest paragraph. Some sections that lend themselves to point form should be set out that way for emphasis, but this format becomes boring when used too often. If your intended audience includes students, headings and sub-headings are very helpful for them.

2. **Content** usually needs modifying too. Beverley Naidoo described recasting her PhD into the book *Through Whose Eyes?* (1992) as 'shearing away' vast sections of text. You no longer have to demonstrate that you are familiar with all the 'authorities' in the field – *you* are now an authority. You cite the others when they support the point *you* are making – or if you want to challenge them. So that's goodbye to Chapter 2 of your thesis – the literature review.

Chapter 1 will almost certainly need to be wholly rewritten. Although it will still introduce the book, it is introducing it to *readers*, not supervisors. And what readers want to know is if this book is going to be relevant, interesting and helpful to *them* and how to find their way around it. So you are still setting out the parameters of the book and indicating how the information is organised but you are also indicating how vital, worthwhile and fascinating that information is.

For much of the remaining chapters you might well be able to download long sections from the PhD and re-edit to the appropriate style. Only if you think that readers will best be led to the conclusions by a different path should you start rearranging the basic order of the chapters or sections. But the conclusion, again, will need major rewriting for your readership and will almost certainly be much briefer.

Follow the instructions on p.36 for the index, take out all references from the original bibliography that are no longer mentioned in the book, give the work a cogent and alluring title with, if you wish, an explanatory sub-title – and there is your book.

Co-authored work

Seldom is it only half the work to write a book with another person. Co-authoring is only justified if combining your knowledge results in a better book.

When people ask at seminars about co-authoring or 'collaborative writing', what they usually want to know about is whose name goes first. This is not as frivolous or self-interested as it seems: for genuinely shared work, it helps if your surname begins with a letter earlier in the alphabet than that of your colleague but the book may well be remembered – as well as cited – as Box and Cox (1999).

With three authors all but the first is likely to be subsumed in '*et al*' and by the time there are four, this is virtually inevitable: think of *Fifteen Thousand Hours (1979)* and you may think only of Rutter; likewise *Teaching about Race Relations; problems and effects* (1982) usually evokes only the name of Stenhouse. All the authors, be there two, three, four or even more, will however be picked up on all databases, and both citations and searches conducted on databases will call up all the authors. Memories are less thorough.

A word of warning about 'with' as in 'by A Box with D Cox and F Knox'. The indexers who create the databases are quite likely to ignore any name that follows 'with', so that Cox and Knox will not appear on the databases. It is an authorship attribution that is best avoided. When the contributors to a book are agreed that one person has done most of the writing, there is no problem about putting that person's name first. Problems arise when two or even three people each feel that they have made the greatest contribution – a not uncommon situation. Agreeing in advance on name order – say, strictly in alphabetical order – can lead to recriminations and ill-feeling later. So do not write with people with whom you cannot negotiate and agree.

Finally you are ready to send your final manuscript to your publisher on disk, in a widely used format, along with an impeccable hard copy. Your publisher should be so completely satisfied that a letter of acceptance and even a first advance on royalties cheque follows immediately. You can expect to respond to the in-house editor's enquiries for several months and then receive page proofs of your work for correcting, using the conventions of proof reading which your publisher will supply. Checking must be done with scrupulous care. Pay particular attention to the names of people you have cited. Errors can be harshly sent up by reviewers and the responsibility is yours.

The index
Unless the corrections involve pagination changes, this is the time to prepare the index. Compiling the index need not be too taxing; your work will be so familiar that you should have few problems. There are books of instruction on indexing, but following the style of other books in the publishing house on your subject may be all you need. You will have already resolved with your editor whether you are doing a subject *and* a citation index, a combined index or simply a subject index. No scholarly

book can be taken seriously if it has no subject index, but citations are negotiable. If other authors want to see if you've quoted them they can check the bibliography – and if they want to know *what* you've quoted, they can read your book!

The subject index has the function of leading readers to the sections that most interest them, and helping them to find these passages again. You will also find it extremely useful yourself when you come to refer to your book a year or two later.

You are now very near the end. Soon you will open your mail to find the very first copy of your book. On opening it your joy will be diminished by immediately spotting an obvious error you missed. Do not let it spoil your day; you are in good company.

Chapters in other people's compilations

Contributing one chapter to a book is no guarantee of citation but it is a good way of getting ideas into print. The drawback is that you might not be consulted about who the other contributors will be and be dismayed to find yourself in certain company. A good academic editor, however, will send out a synopsis of the whole book so that you can also see how your piece fits. It might even be possible to see drafts of the chapters that relate most closely to yours. Working with an experienced editor is your best insurance that your chapter – and the book – will do you credit.

References

Naidoo, B (1992) *Through Whose Eyes*. Stoke on Trent: Trentham Books

Rutter, M, Maughan, B, Mortimore, P and Ouston, J with Smith, A (1979) *Fifteen Thousand Hours: secondary schools and their effects on children.* London: Open Books

Stenhouse, L, Verma, G, Wild, R and Nixon, J (1982) *Teaching about race relations: problems and effects.* London: Routledge and Kegan Paul

CHAPTER 5

Making the most of your publication

As an established author of a learned or professional journal article or a book, you need to exploit your success. The publication may be so outstanding that the world will discover it and rush to read it without any further effort on your part – but this is unlikely. To turn your publication into an asset a new round of effort is required.

The first step is to make all significant colleagues aware of your publication. This involves sending copies of your article, with your signature and compliment slips, very widely. Most journals will provide 50 off-prints free or at a small charge, if they are ordered at the time of acceptance of the article. Make sure you order them. Many journals will bind them in a replica of the actual journal cover. In the case of a book, your publisher will distribute promotional copies for you in the hope that significant members of your field will endorse the book and recommend purchase and even list it as an essential text for their students. Publishers will also ask you for a list of journals to which copies should be sent for review. But if you have supportive colleagues who have good contacts with review editors it is often possible to ask them directly to offer a review of your book to a journal. This technique is still useful if your achievement is an article; encouraging others in your field to cite it or even quote from it is a useful strategy and you should now be in a position to be able to reciprocate in the future.

It may well be that your writing has a wider news value and that local, regional or national media may find in it a 'story' of interest. But they are unlikely to respond to your published text. You require a press release. This is best done in the style of the medium targeted; a range of versions may be needed. Writing a press release is not easy; a good example which reported a research project which later became an article was reprinted in *Research Intelligence* (1996). The first paragraph of the original research summary and the ensuing press release of the ESRC funded project on 'Changing Primary Teachers' Work in England and France' are reproduced here with permission.

> In the last few years primary education in both England and France has been subject to a series of major policy reforms which have had considerable implications for teachers' work and as a result for their pupils' classroom experience. In France, the Jospin reforms (*loi d'orientation sur l'education* 1989) were designed to make primary teachers more responsive to the different learning needs of their pupils and to adopt more individualised, child-responsive approaches to teaching. In England, the emphasis of the Education Reform Act 1988 was rather different, introducing a National Curriculum and national assessment procedures and leading to pressures to adopt a more subject-based approach and more whole class teaching methods to the beliefs of teachers in the two countries.

This research summary was turned into a press release. We reprint the first paragraph to illustrate the contrast. (The release concluded with full information about how to contact the authors for further information and interviews.)

PARTNERSHIP IS THE KEY TO EFFECTIVE REFORM

Research in British and French schools clearly shows the need for education policy-makers to consult more closely, work in partnership with classroom teachers and provide resources and support for change if reform is to be truly effective.

Media response was substantial and widespread, though not always positive. It is possible that none of this response would have occurred without this press release. Sometimes the funding body that supported you will wish to issue its own press release which may not always agree with your own spin, as Brumfit and Mitchell (1996) make painfully clear.

Once your work is more widely known much can follow. Recognition in one's institution is likely to be enhanced; invitations to local staff seminars, key contributions to other and more advanced courses are all to be welcomed. Versions of the publication may be offered as conference papers, which are commonly peer refereed in a similar manner to the original paper; however your contribution is now underwritten in status by its published version. Frequently conference papers are subsequently published in edited volumes; if your paper has been edited, revised and up-dated for the conference, it can be legitimately presented in such a collection with, of course, due acknowledgement to the original version.

A range of opportunities may follow such exposure. Your chances of a successful bid for research funding in your field are enhanced; evidence of ability to achieve publication is an important criterion for most research funding bodies.

Book publishers and their editors are regularly trawling for new authors – invitations, often over expense-paid lunches, are likely to follow if your article has hit the headlines. Enjoy them, but don't over-commit yourself, even though the cash advances may be seductive. Quality rather than quantity of delivery is the key to consolidation and further achievement.

There is the possibility of some further income from your articles in learned journals as well as from your books. Educational establishments in most countries are now required to pay a fee for photocopying of print material. If your work is photocopied you are entitled to part of that fee. To obtain it you must register with the Authors' Licencing and Collecting Society at 74 New Oxford Street, London WC1A 1EF. If you have written a book you should also register with Public Lending Rights Registrar at Bayheath House, Prince Regent Street, Stockton-on-Tees, Cleveland TS18 1DF. This will ensure that you receive a fee based on the estimated number of times your book is borrowed at public libraries.

Once you have become a successful author you may consider using a literary agent. Though agents usually specialise in mass market fiction they are often willing to act for best-selling – or potentially best-selling – academics. The task of the agent is to maximise your income by obtaining the most rewarding contracts from publishers, ensuring that your books are translated and published in other languages, being alert to reproduction of your work in other publications and claiming fees, arranging media appearances and a host of other similar tasks. All your income will have to be assigned to your agent and you will receive all future payments from your agent less an agreed percentage – usually between 10% and 15% – plus the value added tax on the percentage. So we are unconvinced about the potential magic of agents.

If all goes well and your string of articles, books and pamphlets is sound and well regarded, you too will be invited to join review bodies, join distinguished editorial boards, edit journals and series of books and become a member of research awarding bodies – in short to be a leader in your academic or professional discipline. At that point you will need to relearn all that this pamphlet has covered in reverse because you will be at the giving rather than the receiving end. You will have achieved power. Use it with compassion and responsibility and it will endure and earn you yet further esteem and status. Continue to write – it becomes progressively easier – but maintain the quality of your work. It will be scrutinised as an example by the upcoming cohorts.

References

Brumfit, C and Mitchell, R (1996) 'Spinning Right out of Control', *Times Higher Education Supplement*, 28 June

Clare, J (1996) 'Teach us what we do not know' London: *Daily Telegraph*, 21 February

Mortimore, P (1992) 'The First Page of Yesterday's News' in Walford, G *Doing Educational Research*. Buckingham: Open University Press

Osborn, M (1994) 'Changing Primary Teachers' Work in England and France' *Research Intelligence* No 56

Not
Like
Me

MARGUERITE
HANN-SYME

ILLUSTRATED BY
SUE HEAP

WALKER
BOOKS

For Lily and Elsie
MHS

For Jacky
SH

First published 2007 by Walker Books Ltd
87 Vauxhall Walk, London SE11 5HJ

2 4 6 8 10 9 7 5 3

Text © 2007 Marguerite Hann-Syme
Illustrations © 2007 Sue Heap

The right of Marguerite Hann-Syme and Sue Heap to be identified as author
and illustrator respectively of this work has been asserted by them in
accordance with the Copyright, Designs and Patents Act 1988

This book has been typeset in Bembo Educational
and Myriad Bold

Printed and bound in China

British Library Cataloguing in Publication Data:
a catalogue record for this book is available from the British Library

ISBN: 978-1-4063-0383-4

www.walker.co.uk